"You'll Shoot Your Eye Out, Kid!"

A Christmas Story Trivia Book

By

Miguel Dante

<u>Other Books by Miguel Dante</u>

They Flew Away

Evangeline, Alive & Well: A Story of Hope in Haiti

Nelson: The Long Journey of a Tiny Hummingbird

Bright, Shiny Things

Table of Contents

In 1983, cast and crew gathered together to create a small-budget film titled *A Christmas Story*. Although they did not know it at the time, the resulting movie would later become one of the most beloved holiday classics of all time. Millions of fans the world over make watching the movie part of their annual Christmas tradition.

The movie, a sweet and simple tale about a young boy's quest for the perfect Christmas present—a Red Ryder BB gun—ranks high along with other timeless classics such as *It's a Wonderful Life,*

White Christmas and *Rudolph the Red-Nosed Reindeer.*

You'll Shoot Your Eye Out, Kid: A Christmas Story Trivia Book is a fun-filled and loving look back at one of the most hilarious and cherished holiday films of all time, and is the perfect game to bring the family together on Christmas morning!

Multiple Choice

1. What was the name of the department store where Ralphie and Randy visited Santa Claus?

A) Neiman-Marcus

B) Higbee's

C) Gimbel's

D) JC Penneys

2. In what Indiana town did the family live?

A) Terre Haute

B) Madison

C) Hohman

D) Kokomo

3. What was the name of the street where the family lived?

A) Cincinnati Street

B) Madison Avenue

C) Broadway Street

D) Cleveland Street

4. What traditional hymn was the choir singing during the opening of the film?

A) "Go Tell It on the Mountain"

B) "The Old, Rugged Cross"

C) "Amazing Grace"

D) "How Great Thou Art"

5. In what magazine did Ralphie place the ad for the BB gun for his mother to discover?

A) *Time*

B) *Look*

C) *Life*

D) *National Geographic*

6. What star was on the cover of the magazine where Ralphie placed the ad?

A) Joan Crawford

B) Bette Davis

C) Katharine Hepburn

D) Shirley Temple

7: *A Christmas Story* is based on what book by Jean Shepherd?

A) *In God We Trust: All Others Pay Cash*

B) *A Fistful of Fig Newtons*

C) *The Ferrari in the Bedroom*

D) *Wanda Hickey's Night of Golden Memories*

8: What was the family's last name?

A) Miller

B) Parker

C) Smith

D) Taylor

9: What was the father's profession?

A) Insurance Salesman

B) Butcher

C) Used Car Salesman

D) Police Officer

10: How much were the "silly puzzles" the father played potentially worth?

A) $500

B) $1000

C) $5000

D) $50,000

11: Actor Peter Billingsley (Ralphie) appeared on what early-1980s "reality series"?

A) *That's Incredible*

B) *In Search Of*

C) *Big Blue Marble*

D) *Real People*

12: What did Ralphie tell his Mother he actually wanted for Christmas to throw her off the scent?

A) Lincoln Logs

B) Tinker Toys

C) A Slinky

D) Football

13: Who was the leader of the gang of bandits Ralphie defeated with his gun in the dream sequence?

A) Black Bart

B) Greybeard

C) Bugsy Siegel

D) Brutus

14: What was the name of the *Lone Ranger's* nephew's horse?

A) Flicka

B) Agamemnon

C) Victor

D) Trigger

15: In what film did actress Melinda Dillon (the Mother) NOT star?

A) *Close Encounters of the Third Kind*

B) *Tootsie*

C) *Harry & The Hendersons*

D) *The Prince of Tides*

16: What classic novel was Ralphie's class studying?

A) *Red Badge of Courage*

B) *Robinson Crusoe*

C) *Treasure Island*

D) *Silas Marner*

17: What was the name of Ralphie's teacher?

A) Mrs. Shields

B) Mrs. Potter

C) Miss Abbott

D) Miss Landon

18: What present did Ralphie give his teacher for Christmas?

A) Perfume

B) a Fruit Basket

C) a Collection of Bath Soaps

D) a Christmas Sweater

19: What nickname did Ralphie give his gun?

A) Teddy Roosevelt

B) Ol' Boy

C) Ol' Blue

D) Deadeye

20: What brand of soap did Ralphie's mom use to wash his mouth?

A) Lifebuoy

B) Dial

C) Irish Spring

D) Lux

Q&A

Give the answer to each question in the space provided:

21: What was the name of the school Ralphie attended?

_____

22: What Christmas carol was the family singing before their car had a flat tire?

_____

23: Who did Ralphie blame for teaching him the "F Word"?

_____

24: The father said the new artificial Christmas trees looked as if they were made out of what item?

_____

25: What was the last name of the family's Hillbilly neighbors?

_____

26: What breed of dog did the neighbors own?

_____

27: What was the topic of the theme Ralphie's class had to write?

_____

28: What color eyes did Ralphie's nemesis Scut Farkus have?

_____

29: What was the name of Scut Farkus' "crummy little toadie"?

_____

30: Ralphie received a secret decoder for what popular radio show?

_____

31: What basic cable network began broadcasting *A Christmas Story* for a continuous 24 hours?

_____

32: What present did Flick say he was going to give his father for Christmas?

_____

33. What animal did the mother make Randy pretend to be so that he would eat his food?

_____

34: Where was the only room in the house "a boy of nine could sit in privacy"?

_____

35: What "contraband" item did all of the school children put in their mouths before greeting their teacher?

_____

36: What was the actual grade Ralphie received on his theme?

_____

37: What item did Ralphie initially agree he wanted for Christmas when asked by Santa?

_____

38: What was the mother doing when she "accidentally" broke the lamp?

_____

39: What was the father doing when the lamp was broken?

_____

40: What "precious" present did Aunt Clara make for Ralphie?

_____

41: On what classic 70s mystery television series did Darren McGavin star?

_____

42: At what time did the department store close?

_____

43: What movie did the strange boy in line at the department store enjoy?

_____

44: What heavy present did the mother drop into the dad's lap on Christmas morning?

_____

45: What present did Randy play with first on Christmas morning?

_____

46: What ornament on the Christmas tree did the father insist on readjusting?

_____

47: What present did both Ralphie and Randy toss aside immediately after opening?

_____

48: What excuse did Ralphie give for causing his injury and breaking his eye glasses?

_____

49: What restaurant did the family eat dinner at after the dogs devoured the Christmas turkey?

_____

50: What Christmas carols did the wait staff at the restaurant mangle?

_____

Finished Product

Provide the missing word to complete the line from the film:

51: Ralphie: "Flick says he saw some

_____ _____ near

Pulaski's candy store." (two words)

52: Narrator: "Randy lay there like a

_____. It was his only defense."

53: Narrator: "They looked at me as if I had

_____ coming out of my ears."

54: The Dad: "There's another one! Oh, he's a

_____, ain't he?"

55: Ralphie: "Adios. But if you do come back,

you'll be pushing up _____."

56: Narrator: "In the heat of battle, my father wove

a _____ of obscenities that, as far as

we know, is still hanging in space over Lake

_____."

57: Department Store Santa: "I hate the smell of

_____."

58: The Dad: "You use up all the

_____ on purpose!"

59: Flick: "You're full of _____ and
so is your old man!"

60: Narrator: "Only one thing in the world could
have dragged me away from the soft glow of

_____ sex in the window."

61: Ralphie: "Be sure to drink your

_____? A crummy commercial?"

62: The Dad: "Chicago Bears, terror of the midway? More like the Chicago

_____, maybe."

63: Department Store Witch: "The chocolate

_____ eats little boys!"

64: The Dad: "Don't anybody move!!! A

_____ is out!"

65: The Mother: "You stay away from that turkey. It's got an hour to cook. You'll get

_____."

66: The Dad: "He looks like a

_____ nightmare!"

67: The Dad: "That son-of-a-bitch would freeze up in the middle of the summer on the

_____!"

68: Narrator: "My kid brother looked like a

_____ about to pop."

69: Narrator: "Some men are Baptists, others Catholics; my father was an

_____man."

70: The Dad: "You mundane

_____!"

71: The Dad: "Oh for cripe's sake, open up that

_____ will ya? Who the hell turned it all the way down, again?"

72: Narrator: "My little brother had not

_____ voluntarily in over three years."

73: Narrator: It was all over - I was dead. What would it be? The guillotine? Hanging? The chair? The rack? The Chinese

_____ _____?" (Two words)

74: Narrator: "Getting ready to go to school was like getting ready for extended

_____ _____." (Two words)

75: Ralphie's Teacher: "Oh! The theme I've been waiting for all my life. Listen to this sentence: "A

Red Ryder BB gun with a _____ in the stock, and this thing which tells time". Poetry. Sheer poetry, Ralph! An A+!"

76: From the Movie's Tagline: "Peace. Harmony.

Comfort and _____... Maybe Next Year."

77: The Father (after opening all the presents):

"Didn't I get a _____ this year?"

78: The Mother (reassuring Randy after Ralphie's fight): "No, I promise, Daddy is not going to

_____ Ralphie!"

79: Department Store Santa: "If Higbee thinks I'm working one minute past 9:00, he can _____ _____ _____. Ho ho ho." (Three words)

80: Mother: "Randy, will you eat? There are starving people in _____."

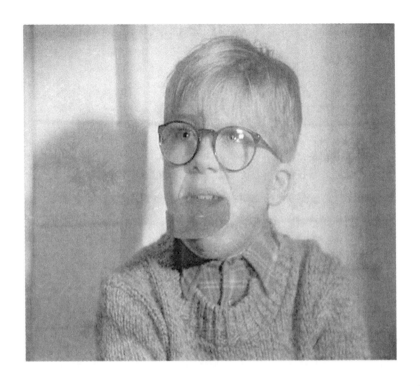

True or False?

Answer each question with a true or false response:

81: The actual house where the movie was filmed is now a museum located in Muncie, Indiana.

_____

82: The actor who portrayed Flick, Scott Schwartz, later appeared in adult movies.

_____

83: Tedde Moore, the actress who played Ralphie's teacher, was actually pregnant at the time the movie was filmed.

_____

84: The Dad thought that the word "Fragile" written on the crate containing his prize was in Spanish.

_____

85: The film was nominated for a Best Picture Academy Award.

_____

86: The Mother had trouble getting Randy to eat his least favorite dish, red cabbage and beans.

_____

87: The family car had a flat tire when Ralphie said the dreaded "F word".

_____

88: The film's sequel, *A Christmas Story 2*, earned more at the box office than the original movie.

_____

89: Darren McGavin portrayed the father to actress Candice Bergen's character on the hit sitcom *Murphy Brown*.

_____

90: The Dad tripped on a slinky while going down the stairs to the basement to repair the furnace.

———————————

91: The town where the movie is set was inspired by author Jean Shepherd's real-life hometown of Hammond, Indiana.

———————————

92: The film's director Bob Clark directed the hit adult comedy *Porky's* before being hired to direct *A Christmas Story*.

———————————

93: Actor Zack Ward, who played Scut Farkus, produced a musical based on the film, "A Christmas Story: A Musical".

———————————

94: The film's author and narrator, Jean Shepherd, does a "Hitchcock" cameo appearance in the movie.

———————————

95: Actress Melinda Dillon appears in the film's sequel, *My Summer Story*.

———————————

96: The film's director, Bob Clark, appeared in the film as one of the family's neighbors.

———————————

97: The carol "O Holy Night" is played during the movie's ending credits.

———————————

98: The film achieved only modest success when it was initially released in 1983.

———————————

99: The movie inspired a Broadway musical as well.

———————————

100: A weekly television sitcom based on the family from the film debuted in the late-1980s.

———————————

The Cast

- Peter Billingsley **as Ralphie**
- Jean Shepherd **as adult Ralphie (Narrator)**
- Ian Petrella **as Randy**
- Darren McGavin **as The Father (The Old Man)**
- Melinda Dillon **as The Mother**
- Scott Schwartz **as Flick**
- R. D. Robb **as Schwartz**
- Zack Ward **as Scut Farkus**
- Yano Anaya **as Grover Dill**
- Tedde Moore **as The Teacher**

The Answers…

Multiple Choice Answers

1: B, Higbees

2: C, Hohman, Indiana

3: D, Cleveland Street

4: A, "Go Tell It on the Mountain"

5: B, *Look* magazine

6: D, Shirley Temple

7: A, *In God We Trust: All Others Pay Cash*

8: B, the Parker Family

9: C, Used car salesman

10: D, $50,000

11: D, *Real People*

12: B, Tinker toys

13: A, Black Bart

14: C, Victor

15: B, *Tootsie*

16: D, *Silas Marner*

17: A, Mrs. Shields

18: B, a fruit basket

19: C, Ol' Blue

20: A, Lifebuoy

Q&A Answers

21: Warren G. Harding Elementary School

22: "Jingle Bells"

23: Schwartz

24: green pipe cleaners

25: the Bumpuses

26: Bloodhounds

27: "What I Want for Christmas"

28: yellow

29: Grover Dill

30: *Little Orphan Annie*

31: TBS

32: a flower that squirts water

33: a pig

34: the bathroom

35: fake teeth

36: C+

37: a football

38: watering her plants

39: repairing the furnace

40: a pink bunny outfit

41: *Kolchak: The Nightstalker*

42: 9:00PM

43: *The Wizard of Oz*

44: a bowling ball

45: a fire truck

46: the star on top of the Christmas tree

47: socks

48: an icicle fell from the garage and knocked his glasses from his face.

49: the Chop Suey Palace

50: "Deck the Halls" and "Jingle Bells"

Finished Product Answers:

51: Grizzly bears

52: slug

53: lobsters

54: dead-eye

55: daisies

56: tapestry, Michigan

57: tapioca

58: glue

59: beans

60: electric

61: Ovaltine

62: chipmunks

63: snowman

64: fuse

65: worms

66: pink

67: equator

68: tick

69: Oldsmobile

70: noodle

71: damper

72: eaten

73: water torture

74: deep-sea diving

75: compass

76: joy

77: tie

78: kill

79: kiss my foot

80: China

True or False Answers:

81: False. The house is indeed now a museum, but it is located in the city of Cleveland, Ohio.

82: True, although briefly.

83: True

84: False. He believed that it was written in Italian.

85: False

86: False. It was the dreaded meatloaf!

87: True

88: False

89: True

90: False. He tripped on a pair of skates as he was going down the stairs.

91: True

92: True

93: False. Peter Billingsley did produce a stage version.

94: True. He played the irate man who yells at Ralphie and Randy for breaking in line to see Santa at the department store.

95: False

96: True

97: False. The carol is "We Wish You a Merry Christmas".

98: True

99: True

100: False

About the Author

Miguel Dante is the bestselling author of the children's books *Evangeline, Alive & Well: A Story of Hope in Haiti* and *They Flew Away.* He also writes his own popular blog, *Too Much Information! With Miguel Dante:* (www.migueldante.com)

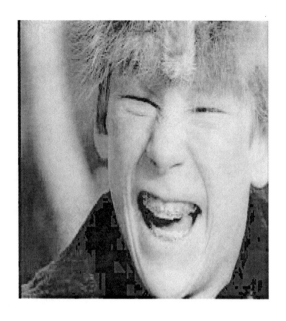

CPSIA information can be obtained
at www.ICGtesting.com
Printed in the USA
LVOW07s0045181217
560124LV00022B/2520/P